Generis
PUBLISHING

AF579358

The Impact of Strategic Response Capabilities on Business Success in Kenya

A case of organizations listed in the Nairobi Securities Exchange

Dr. Peter Kiboi Ngugi

Title: **The Impact of Strategic Response Capabilities on Business Success in Kenya**

A case of organizations listed in the Nairobi Securities Exchange

ISBN: 979-8-89248-648-4

Author: Dr. Peter Kiboi Ngugi

Cover image: https://pixabay.com/

Publisher: Generis Publishing
Online orders: www.generis-publishing.com
Contact email: info@generis-publishing.com

THE INFLUENCE OF STRATEGIC COMPETITIVE RESPONSE CAPABILITY ON THE PERFORMANCE OF COMMERCIAL ORGANIZATIONS IN KENYA LISTED IN NAIROBI SECURITIES EXCHANGE

Dr. Peter K. Ngugi Business Development and Consultancy Services Manager

Kenya Utalii College, P. Box 31052-00600 Nairobi

TABLE OF CONTENTS

ABSTRACT

Strategic competitive response has been identified as effective factor that harnesses a business ability to utilize all its skills, capabilities and resources in order to gain competitive advantage and thus survive and increase its value over time. It focuses on the organization's assets, resources and market position, projecting how well it will be able to employ strategies in the future. This study sought to explore the influence of strategic competitive response capability deployment on performance of listed organizations in Nairobi securities exchange. There is a dearth of studies empirically investigating the relationship between interaction of strategic competitive response capability deployment and organizational performance. This gap in knowledge is exacerbated by multiple definitions, ambiguity of constructs, contradicting views and little grounding of the theory in empirical observation. The objective was to determine the influence of strategic response capability performance. The study employed two theories to explain the interaction of strategic competitive response action and organizational performance, the theories were resource-based view and dynamic capabilities theory. A cross sectional research design was employed with the focus set on the operations of corporations listed in Nairobi securities exchange. A census survey of 67 firms was conducted. The results show that strategic competitive response has a positive statistically significant relationship with performance ($\beta=0.600$, $p=.000$). The results have also shown that strategic competitive response was positively correlated to organizational performance at 99% confidence level ($r=6.45$, $p=0.000$).This study concludes that strategic competitive response capability significantly influences organizational performance positively. The findings of this study would help firms listed in the Nairobi Securities Exchange identify critical factors and design sustainable strategies to improve their strategic competitive response capability through strategic planning and ensuring that they are up to date with modern trends in technology and other information related to their industry.

INTRODUCTION

Organizational Performance can be seen as a measure of how efficiently and effectively managers use available resources to satisfy customers and achieve organizational goals. Two words are important in this matter, Efficiency and Effectiveness; efficiency being a measure of how well or how productively resources are used to achieve a goal, while effectiveness is seen as a measure of the appropriateness of the goals an organization is pursuing and the degree to which they are achieved. According to Ibraimi (2014), the relationship between strategy and performance can contribute to greater effectiveness for individual firms and entire economies.

Reviewing past studies reveals a multidimensional conceptualization of organizational performance related predominately to stakeholders, heterogeneous product market circumstances, and time. A review of the operationalization of performance highlights the limited effectiveness of commonly accepted measurement practices in tapping this multidimensionality. Addressing these findings requires researchers to possessing a strong theoretical rationale on the nature of performance i.e., theory establishing which measures are appropriate to the research context and relying on strong theory as to the nature of measures of the theory establishing which measures should be combined and the method for doing so (Bryant & Widener 2004).

The primary focus of strategic management as a body of knowledge is how organizations generate and sustain advantage (Abrosini and Bowwan, 2000). Most strategic management studies have measured performance using conventional measures of economic prosperity, based on shareholders approach. The two most popular measure related to economic prosperity of performance are return on assets and growth in sales.

Strategic Competitive Response Capability deployment

Strategic competitive response capability is based on the extended definition of dynamic capabilities proposed by Wang and Ahmed (2007) to include the creation of market change as well as the response to exogenous change (Helfat et al., 2007). This capability can be conceptualized as the ability of the firm to scan the environment, identify new opportunities, asses its competitive position and respond to competitive strategic moves. Even when a wellestablished firm is aware of a need for change to address shifting environmental requirements, it is often difficult to respond effectively. For example, empirical research provides evidence that changes related to even minor technology shifts are often hard to be addressed effectively. However, the capability to sense and strategically respond to environmental challenges is of utmost importance as it enables the firm to reconfigure certain competences before they become core rigidities (Teece, 2010; Frese, 2008).

In choosing what moves their firms, executives have to decide whether to respond to moves made by rivals. Figuring out how to react, if at all, to a competitor's move ranks among the most challenging decisions that executives must make. Research indicates that three factors determine the likelihood that a firm will respond to a competitive move: awareness, motivation, and capability. These three factors together determine the level of competition tension that exists between rivals

Awareness is a statement that must be found primarily for competitive actions and responses taken by the company or competitors, and includes the extent to which competitors are aware of the degree of interdependence as a result of resource similarity and market partnerships (Hitt et al., 2005). Awareness also refers to the awareness of the company, its competitors, the competitive elements in the industry, and the competitive environment. The level of awareness is very important because it affects the level and conception of conclusions about the results of the company's actions in a competitive environment (Smith et al., 2001). Motivation comes from the Latin word movere which means drive or driving force. In management it is only aimed at human resources in general and in particular subordinates (Purba and Sudibjo, 2020). Motivation involves the incentives offered by the company to move or respond to rush opponents in relation to perceived advantages and disadvantages (Ireland, et al, 2011). The company may be aware of its competitors, but if you see that the movement of competitors will not have a negative impact on the company, the motivation to enter competition with competitors will be low (Hitt et al, 2005). In his research on competitive dynamics, he noted that organizational characteristics such as past performance and market dependence (Heuermann, 2005), reflect motivation to move (Smith et al., 2001). A company with high market dependence will be more aggressive in maintaining its market position (Heuermann, 2005).

Capability is about the resources of each company and the flexibility required they give. Without the right resources (such as capital and people), the company will not have the capability to make moves or respond to its actions (Hitt et al, 2005). However, similar resources will bring about similar capabilities for movement and response (Chen, 1996).

STUDY METHODOLOGY

The study was done through a census survey of commercial organizations listed at the Nairobi securities Exchange. The target population was 67 the whole population of listed companies. Four questionnaires were administered in each of the firms, making the sample population to be 268. The questionnaires were dropped to four heads of strategic business units that included finance, operations, corporate communication and human resources. The questionnaires were administered using drop-and-pick later method that facilitated ample time to respond. The questionnaire was divided into 3 categories general information and the following variables, competitive strategic response, performance measurement. Primary data was collected through semi structured questionnaire with 5- point Likert-style scale strongly agree disagree questionnaire. The unit of analysis was commercial organizations listed in Nairobi Securities Exchange because the study was to identify the influence of strategic competitive response capabilities deployment, and performance for commercial organizations listed in Nairobi Securities Exchange. The research was cross sectional as the data was gathered just once over a period of months. Analysis was done using descriptive and inferential statistics that entailed linear regression and correlation analysis that yielded coefficients for interpretation and making conclusions. The following regression model was used in data analysis.

Models 1: $Y=\beta 0+ \beta 1X+ \varepsilon$

Where;

Y: Is the Organizational Performance $\beta 0$: is Constant terms for corresponding variables

X1: Strategic competitive response capability deployment ε: is the error term

Strategic Competitive Response capability

The respondents were asked to indicate their level of agreement or disagreement with statements regarding strategic competitive response and they used a likert scale of 1-5 where 1 was strongly disagree, 2 disagree, 3 neutral, 4 agree and 5 strongly agree. The results show that respondents were neutral on the statement that their organization embraces strategic planning in its every day operations (58.1%). The results also show that majority of the respondents agreed with the statements that their organization engages in active intelligence gathering to retain competitive position (62.1%) and that their organization reviews and upgrades its products regularly (50.2%). Majority of the respondents agreed with the statements that strategy is clearly translated into organizational, departmental, unit and individual goals and objectives (55.7%), that their organization is flexible to adaptation of new industry and market trends (59.1%) and that their organization supports R&D to maintain competitiveness and work on progress regularly (60.1%).

The results in table 4.5 shows that overall, respondents agreed with the statements that the management of the organization believes in continuous planning, fast collection and analysis of market information to always accomplish more for the team success (M=4.32, SD=.710). The findings also show that overall respondents agreed also with the statements that their organization reviews and upgrades its products regularly (M=4.12, SD=.696), strategy is clearly translated into organizational, departmental, unit and individual goals and objectives (M=4.24, SD=.713) and that their organization is flexible to adaptation of new industry and market trends (M=4.17, SD=.654).

Table 4. 1: Descriptive Statistics for Strategic Competitive Response Capability Factors

Minimu Maximu Mean Std	Skewness Statistic	Kurtosis Statistic	M Statistic	M Statistic	Deviation Statistic	Statistic Std.	Error Statistic	Std. Error
Our organization embraces strategic technological trends in the industry planning in its every day operations	1	5	3.43	.710	.171	.171	1.281	.340
My organization engages in active intelligence gathering to retain competitive position	3	5	3.90	.609	.054	.171	-.325	.340
The management of the organization believes in continuous planning, fast collection and analysis of market information to always accomplish more for the team success	2	5	4.32	.710	-.792	.171	.301	.340
My organization reviews and	3	5	4.12	.696	-.171	.171	-.924	.340

upgrades its products regularly								
Strategy is clearly translated into organizational, departmental, unit and individual goals and objectives.								
The organization deeply is up to date with the	1	5	4.24	.713	-1.373	.171	4.638	.340
	2	5	3.99	.738	-.134	.171	-.748	.340
This organization is flexible to adaptation of industry and market new trends	2	5	4.17	.654	-.507	.171	.651	.340
My organization supports R&D to maintain competitiveness and work on progress regularly	1	5	3.96	.720	-.900	.171	2.810	.340

Factor Analysis Results

Factor analysis was done for the variables of the study. The factor analysis results of the variables are presented. These variables include strategic competitive response, and organizational performance.

Strategic Competitive Response Capability deployment

The results show that two factors underlie strategic competitive response capability deployment. These two factors were extracted as they have an eigenvalue of 1.0 or higher. The results in table 4.12 show that the first factor explains 32.8% while the second factor explains 20.7% of strategic competitive response. The two factors cumulatively explains 53.5% of variation in strategic competitive response.

Table 4. 2: Total Variance Explained for Strategic Competitive Response Capability deployment Factors

Component	Initial Eigenvalues			Extraction Sums of Squared Loadings			Rotation Sums of Squared Loadings		
	Total	% of Variance	Cumulative %	Total	% of Variance	Cumulative %	Total	% of Variance	Cumulative %
1	2.622	32.779	32.779	2.622	32.779	32.779	2.148	26.854	26.854
2	1.655	20.688	53.467	1.655	20.688	53.467	2.129	26.613	53.467
3	.929	11.607	65.074						
4	.802	10.029	75.103						
5	.677	8.456	83.559						
6	.507	6.343	89.903						
7	.434	5.419	95.322						
8	.374	4.678	100.000						

Table 4.13 shows that four items loaded high on the first factor. They included strategy is clearly translated into organizational, departmental, unit and individual goals and objectives (.780), my organization supports R&D to maintain competitiveness and work on progress regularly (.738), this organization is flexible to adaptation of new industry and market trends (.647) and our organization embraces strategic planning in its every day operations (.642). The items that loaded high on the second factor included the statements that the organization deeply is up to date with the technological trends in the industry (.809), my organization reviews and upgrades its products regularly (.710), the management of the organization believes in continuous planning, fast collection and analysis of market information to always accomplish more for the team success (.692) and that my organization engages in active intelligence gathering to retain competitive position (.426). Based on the items that loaded high on the two factors, the first factor is strategic planning while the second factor is state-of-the-art trends in technology and information in the industry.

Table 4. 3: Rotated Component Matrix for Strategic Competitive Response Factors

	Component	
	1	2
Strategy is clearly translated into organizational, departmental, unit and individual goals and objectives.	.780	
My organization supports R&D to maintain competitiveness and work on progress regularly	.738	
This organization is flexible to adaptation of new industry and market trends	.647	
Our organization embraces strategic planning in its every day operations	.642	
The organization deeply is up to date with the technological trends in the industry		.809
My organization reviews and upgrades its products regularly		.710
The management of the organization believes in continuous planning, fast collection and analysis of market information to always accomplish more for the team success		.692
My organization engages in active intelligence gathering to retain competitive position		

Extraction Method: Principal Component Analysis
Rotation Method: Varimax with Kaiser Normalization.[a]

. a. Rotation converged in 3 iterations.

The Kaiser-Meyer-Olkin Measure of Sampling Adequacy is 0.694 which is average and shows that patterns of correlations are relatively compact and so factor analysis should yield distinct and reliable factors. Factor analysis was therefore appropriate for these data. The Bartlett's Test of Sphericity is highly significant ($p< 0.000$), and therefore factor analysis is appropriate.

KMO and Bartlett's Test

Kaiser-Meyer-Olkin Measure of Sampling Adequacy.		.694
Bartlett's Test of Sphericity	Approx. Chi-Square	340.277
	df	28
	Sig.	.000

Organizational Performance

The results show that three factors underlie organizational performance. These three factors were extracted as they have an eigen value of 1.0 or higher. The results in table 4.16 show that the first factor explained 25.6% of variation in organizational performance while the second factor explained 16% of variation in organizational performance. The third factor explained 13.4% of variation in organizational performance. Cumulatively, the three factors explained 55% of variance in organizational performance.

Table 4. 4: Total Variance Explained for Organizational Performance Factors

Component	Initial Eigenvalues			Extraction Sums of Squared Loadings			Rotation Sums of Squared Loadings		
	Total	% of Variance	Cumulative %	Total	% of Variance	Cumulative %	Total	% of Variance	Cumulative %
1	2.050	25.629	25.629	2.050	25.629	25.629	1.509	18.862	18.862
2	1.283	16.035	41.663	1.283	16.035	41.663	1.459	18.238	37.100
3	1.070	13.378	55.041	1.070	13.378	55.041	1.435	17.941	55.041
4	.989	12.356	67.398						
5	.883	11.037	78.435						
6	.718	8.976	87.411						
7	.639	7.993	95.404						
8	.368	4.596	100.000						

Results in table 4.17, shows that three items loaded high in the first factor, another three in the second factor and four in the third factor. The items that loaded high on the first factor included statements that customers' needs are responded to swiftly (.825), the organization has gained new customers recently (.658) and the organization observes delivery on-time and on specification to its customers (.469). The items that loaded high on the second factor included the statements that the organization has gained new customers recently (.406), the company's customer groups and market segments are clearly defined and selected (.823) and the organization has a high customer retention (.692). The items that loaded high on the third factor included the statements that the organization has a high customer retention (.359), there are processes to improve efficiency (.772), the organization has achieved the image of a trusted supplier (.719) and there are new products and services based on customer needs (.391). Based on the items that loaded high on the factors, the first factor can be deduced to be customer focus while the second and third factors are customer loyalty and efficient processes respectively. Table 4. 5: Rotated Component Matrix for Organizational Performance Factors

	Component		
	1	2	3
Customers' needs are responded to swiftly	.825		
The organization has gained new customers recently	.658		
The organization observes delivery on-time and on specification to its customers			
The company's customer groups and market segments are clearly defined and	.823	salected	
The organization has a high customer retention	.692		
There are processes to improve efficiency	.772		
The organization has achieved the image of a trusted supplier		.719	
There are new products and services based on customer needs	.391		
Extraction Method: Principal Component Analysis. Rotation Method: Varimax with Kaiser Normalization.[a]			

a. Rotation converged in 6 iterations.

The Kaiser-Meyer-Olkin Measure of Sampling Adequacy is 0.495 which is close to 0.5 hence average and shows that patterns of correlations are relatively compact and so factor analysis should yield distinct and reliable factors. Factor analysis was therefore appropriate for these data.

The Bartlett's Test of Sphericity is highly significant (p< 0.000), and therefore factor analysis is appropriate.

KMO and Bartlett's Test		
Kaiser-Meyer-Olkin Measure of Sampling Adequacy.		.495
Bartlett's Test of Sphericity	Approx. Chi-Square	174.683
	df	28
	Sig.	.000

Conceptual Model key effects on Hypotheses

To determine the effect of strategic competitive response on performance, the relevant null hypotheses was postulated as follows:

H_1: Strategic competitive response capability does not influence organizational performance of Organizations in Kenya listed at Nairobi securities.

Model

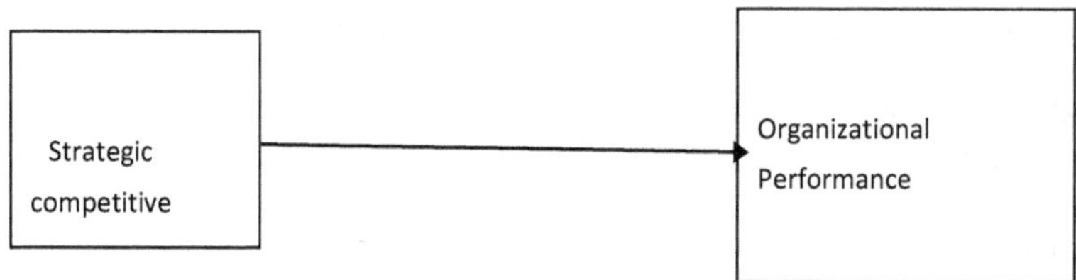

Source: Researcher, 2015

Correlation Analysis

A correlation analysis was done to establish the relationship between the independent variables and dependent variables. The results show that strategic competitive response capability deployment was positively correlated to organizational performance at 99% confidence level (r=.645, $p=0.000$). These findings show a direct relationship between strategic competitive response and organizational performance in that the higher the level of strategic competitive response, the higher the organizational performance

Table 4. 6: Correlations Analysis

		Strategic	Organizational	Response	Competitive	Performance
Strategic Response capability	Pearson . Sig. (2-tailed)			competitive deployment	Correlation N	203
			.703**			
Organizational performance	Pearson Correlation Sig. (2-tailed) N		203	.645 ** .000 203		

**. Correlation is significant at the 0.01 level (2-tailed).

Hypothesis Testing

Simple linier regression analysis was done to test the study hypothesisH_1 The model used for analysis is Y=β0+ β1X1+ ε. The results presented in table 4.19 show that predictor variables strategic competitive response, explain 45.7% of change in dependent variable organizational performance (R^2=.457).

Table 4. 7: Model Summary

Model	R	R Square	Adjusted R Square	Std. Error of the Estimate
1	.682a	.465	.457	1.27661

a. Predictors: (Constant), Strategic competitive Response.

Analysis of variance (ANOVA) was used to test the fitness of the analysis model. The results of F value show that the analysis model used was fit and the results obtained were significant hence did not occur by chance (F=57.612, *p=.000*). These results are shown in table 4.20.

Table 4. 8: ANOVA

Model		Sum of Squares	df	Mean Square	F	Sig.
1	Regression	281.681	3	93.894	57.612	.000b
	Residual	324.319	199	1.630		
	Total	606.000	202			

a. Dependent Variable: Organizational Performance

b. Predictors: (Constant), Strategic Competitive Response, Coordination, Organizational Learning

The coefficients shown in table 4.21 indicate that strategic competitive response capability deployment contributed to organizational performance by a factor of 0.6 (β=.600, *p=.000*). Strategic competitive response capability deployment has a statistically significant contribution to organizational performance. The results mean that we reject the third hypothesis H_3 *strategic competitive response capability deployment has no significant relationship with organizational performance*. These results are shown in table 4.21.

Table 4. 9: Coefficients

Model	Unstandardized Coefficients		Standardized Coefficients	t	Sig.
	B	Std. Error	Beta		
(Constant)	-5.613	.090		.000	1.000
Strategic Competitive Response	.600	.085	.490	7.066	.000

a. Dependent Variable: Organizational performance

Tables 4.19 and 4.21 summarize these findings. These results of simple linear regression have illustrated that strategic competitive response capabilities deployment explain 45.7% of change in dependent variable organizational performance (R^2=.457).

DISCUSSION

The objective of the study was to determine the influence of strategic competitive response capability deployment on the performance of commercial organizations in Kenya listed in Nairobi Securities Exchange. The hypothesis *H01 Strategic competitive response capability deployment has no significant relationship with organizational performance* was tested. The results show that strategic competitive response has a positive statistically significant relationship with organizational performance hence the study rejected null hypothesis. The better, the strategic competitive response capability deployment by the organization better the organizational performance. Strategic planning and state-of-the-art trends in technology and information in the industry are the two important elements of strategic competitive response. The results show that strategic competitive response capability deployment has a positive statistically significant relationship with organizational performance. The better the strategic competitive response capability deployment, the better the organizational performance.

CONCLUSION AND IMPLICATION

This study concludes that strategic planning and state-of-the-art trends in technology and information in the industry are two important pointers of strategic competitive response for organizations. The study also concludes that strategic competitive response significantly influences organizational performance of firms listed at the Nairobi Securities Exchange. The higher the strategic competitive response capability a firm has, the better the organizational performance. These results are in agreement with argument by (Helfat, 2007) described strategic competitive response as the ability of the firm to scan the environment, identify new opportunities, assess its competitive position and respond to competitive strategic moves. (Teece, 2007) and (Frese, 2008) also emphasized on the capability to sense and strategically respond to environmental challenges. They observed that this capability is of utmost importance to organizational performance as it enables the firm to reconfigure certain competences before they become core rigidities. The study as well agrees with (Katkalo et al., 2010), strategy as sensing being recognition of market and technological opportunities and the mobilization of requisite resources. The study also postulates that strategic competitive response enhances information processing, hence issues are identified and appropriate responses taken much sooner than would otherwise be the case in the firms strategic planning process as according to (Ibid, 1995). These also collaborates empirical studies observing that fast decision makers collect more information and develop more alternatives than do the slow decision makers (Eisenhardt, 1989).

REFERENCES

Adner, R., &Helfat, C. E. (2003). Corporate effects and dynamic managerial capabilities. *Strategic Management Journal*, *24*(10), 1011-1025.

Allred, C.R., Fawcett, S.E., Wallin, C. &Magnan, G.M. (2011). A dynamic collaboration capability as a source of competitive advantage, *Decision Sciences*, 42(1), pp. 129.161.

Ambrosini, V., & Bowman, C. (2009). What are dynamic capabilities and are they a useful construct in strategic management?*International Journal of Management Reviews*, *11*(1), 29-49.

Amit, R., &Schoemaker, P. J. (1993). Strategic assets and organizational rent. *Strategic management journal*, *14*(1), 33-46.

Archer, M. S. (1995). *Realist social theory: The morphogenetic approach*. Cambridge university press.

Baard, S.K., Rench, T.A., Kozlowski, S.W.J. (2014). Performance adaptation: a theoretical integration and review. *Journal of Management*, 40, pp. 48–99.

Bajpai, N. (2011). *Business Research Methods*. Pearson Education: New Delhi, India.

Banterle, A., & Carraresi L. (2007). Competitive performance analysis and European Union trade: The case of the prepared swine meat sector. *Food Economics – ActaAgriculturaeScandinavica Section C*, 4(3), pp. 159-172.

Barney, J. B. (1991). Firm resources and sustained competitive advantage. *Journal of Management*, 17, pp. 99-120.

Barreto, I. (2010). Dynamic Capabilities: A Review of Past Research and an Agenda for the Future. *Journal of Management*, 36(1), pp.256-280.

Belleflamme, P. & Peitz, M. (2010). *Industrial Organization: Markets and Strategies*. Cambridge: Cambridge University Press.

Bowman, C. & Ambrosini, V. (2009). What are dynamic capabilities and are they a useful construct in strategic management? *International Journal of Management Reviews*, 11(1), pp. 29–49.

Campbell, J.P. & Wiernik, B.M. (2015). The Modeling and Assessment of Work Performance. The *Annual Review of Organizational Psychology and Organizational Behavior*, 2, pp. 47-74.

Cardeal, N., & Antonio, N. S. (2012). Valuable, rare, inimitable resources and organization (VRIO) resources or valuable, rare, inimitable resources (VRI) capabilities: What leads to competitive advantage?*Cardeal, N., António*, (2012), 10159-10170.

Carraresi, L., Mamaqi, X., Albisu, L.M. & Banterle, A. (2011). The relationship between strategic choices and performance in Italian food SMEs: a resource-based approach. *Paper prepared for presentation at the EAAE 2011 Congress, Change and Uncertainty; Challenges for Agriculture, Food and Natural Resources* August 30 to September 2, 2011 ETH Zurich, Zurich, Switzerland.

Cepeda, G., & Vera, D. (2007). Dynamic capabilities and operational capabilities: A knowledge management perspective. *Journal of Business Research*, *60*(5), 426-437.

Chenhall, R. H., & Langfield-Smith, K. (2007). Multiple perspectives of performance measures. *European Management Journal*, *25*(4), 266-282.

.........(2007). Multiple perspectives of performance measures. *European Management Journal*, *25*(4), 266-282.

Eisenhardt, K. M., & Martin, J. A. (2000). Dynamic capabilities: what are they?.*Strategic management journal*, *21*(10-11), 1105-1121.

Gachanja, P.M., Etyang, M.N., &Wawire, N.H.W. (2008). Total Factor Productivity Change in the Kenya Manufacturing Sector: A Malmquist Index Analysis. Unpublished Paper, Kenyatta University.

Gelfand, M. J., Erez, M., &Aycan, Z. (2007). Cross-cultural organizational behavior. *Annu. Rev. Psychol.*, *58*, 479-514.

Helfat, C. E., &Peteraf, M. A. (2003). The dynamic resource-based view: Capability lifecycles. *Strategic management journal*, *24*(10), 997-1010.

……… (2009). Understanding dynamic capabilities: progress along a developmental path. *Strategic organization*, *7*(1), 91.

Helfat, C. E., Finkelstein, S., Mitchell, W., Peteraf, M., Singh, H., Teece, D., &Winter, S. G. (2009). *Dynamic capabilities: Understanding strategic change in organizations*. John Wiley & Sons.

Hubbard, G. (2009). Measuring organizational performance: beyond the triple bottom line. *Business strategy and the environment*, *18*(3), 177-191.

Ibraimi, S. (2014). Performance Determinants of Manufacturing Firms: Analysis from a Strategic Management Perspective. *International Journal of Academic Research in Economics and Management Sciences*, 3(2), pp. 92-112.

Kaplan, R. S. & Norton, D.P. (2008). *The Execution Premium: Linking Strategy to Operations for Competitive Advantage*, Boston: HBS Press.

Kaplan, R.S. (2010). Conceptual Foundations of the Balanced Scorecard, *Working Paper 10-074*, Harvard Business School, Harvard University.

Karanja, S.,Muathe, S.M.A. &Thuo, J. (2014). The Effect of Marketing Capabilities and Distribution Strategy on Performance of MSP Intermediary Organizations' in Nairobi County, Kenya. *Business Management and Strategy,* Vol. 5, No. 1

Klein, P.G., Mahoney, J.T., McGahan, A.M. & Pitelis, C.N. (2010). Resources, Capabilities, and Routines in Public Organizations. Rotman School of Management *Working Paper No. 1550028; Atlanta Competitive Advantage Conference 2010 Paper*. Available at SSRN: https://ssrn.com/abstract=1550028

Klein, P. G., Mahoney, J. T., McGahan, A. M., &Pitelis, C. N. (2013). Capabilities and strategic entrepreneurship in public organizations. *Strategic Entrepreneurship Journal*, *7*(1), 70-91.

Lings, I., Wilden, R., &Gudergan, S. (2009). The effects of sensing and seizing of market opportunities and reconfiguring activities on the organisational resource base. In *Proceedings of Australian and New Zealand Marketing Academy Conference 2009*. ANZMAC.

Liu, C.M. (2007). The early employment influences of sales representatives on the development of organizational commitment, *Employee Relations*, 29(1), pp. 5-15.

Lo, Y. H. (2012). Managerial Capabilities, Organizational Culture and Organizational Performance: The resource-based perspective in Chinese lodging industry. *Journal of International Management Studies*, *7*(1), 151.

Ludwig, G. & Pemberton, J. (2011). A managerial perspective of dynamic capabilities in emerging markets: the case of the Russian steel industry, *Journal of East European Management Studies*, 16(3), pp. 215–236.

Mangos, P.M., Arnold, R.D. (2008). Enhancing military training through the application of maximum and typical performance measurement principles. *Performance Improvement*, 47, pp. 29–35.

Moliterno, T. P., &Wiersema, M. F. (2007). Organizational performance, rent appropriation, and the strategic resource divestment capability. *Strategic Management Journal*, *28*(11), 1065-1087.

Mugambi, G.K, Chege, J.M &K'Obonyo, P. (2011). PIMS and Corporate Performance: The Influence of Strategic Capabilities and Contextual factors in Kenya. Unpublished Paper, Kenyatta University.

Newbert, S. L. (2008), Value, rareness, competitive advantage, and performance: A conceptual-level empirical investigation of the resource-based view of the firm, *Strategic Management Journal*, 29, pp.745-768.

Penrose, E. T. (1995). The theory of the growth of the firm, 1959. *Cambridge, MA*.

Porter, M.E. & Heppelmann, J.E. (2015). How Smart, Connected Products are Transforming Companies, *Harvard Business Review*, October 2015, pp. 97—114.

Priem, R. L., & Butler, J. E. (2001). Is the resource-based "view" a useful perspective for strategic management research?. *Academy of management review*, *26*(1), 22-40.

Richard, P. J., Devinney, T. M., Yip, G. S., & Johnson, G. (2009). Measuring organizational performance: Towards methodological best practice. *Journal of management*.

Rose, R.C., Abdullah, H. &Ismad, A.I. (2010). A Review on the Relationship between Organizational Resources, Competitive Advantage and Performance. *The Journal of International Social Research*, 3(11), pp. 488-498.

Santos, J. & Brito, L. (2012). Toward a Subjective Measurement Model for Firm Performance. *Brazilian Administration Review,* 9(6), pp. 95-117.

Saunders, M., Lewis, P. & Thornhill, A. (2012). *Research Methods for Business Students*, 6th edition. Pearson Education: New Delhi, India.

Sonnentag, S., Volmer, J. & Spychala, A. (2010). *Job Performance: Sage handbook of organizational behavior.* Los Angeles: SAGE.

Talaja, A. (2012). Testing VRIN framework: Resource value and rareness as sources of competitive advantage and above average performance. *Management: Journal of Contemporary Management Issues*, *17*(2), 51-64.

Teece, David J. (2010). Technological Innovation and the Theory of the Firm: The Role of Enterprise-level Knowledge, Complementarities, and (Dynamic) Capabilities. In N. Rosenberg and B. Hall (eds.) *Handbook of the Economics of Innovation*. Amsterdam: North-Holland.

Teece, D.J. (2007). Explicating Dynamic Capabilities: The Nature and Microfoundations of (Sustainable) Enterprise Performance. *Strategic Management Journal. John Wiley & Sons*. 28 (13), pp. 1319– 1350.

Teece, D. J. (2007). Explicating dynamic capabilities: the nature and microfoundations of (sustainable) enterprise performance. *Strategic management journal*, *28*(13), 1319-1350.

Venkatraman, N., & Ramanujam, V. (1986). Measurement of business performance in strategy research: A comparison of approaches. *Academy of management review*, *11*(4), 801-814.

Waiganjo, E., Mukulu, E. &Khariri, J. (2012). Relationship between Strategic Human Resource Management & Firm Performance of Kenya's Corporate Organizations. *International Journal of Humanities & Social Science*. 2(10), 62-70.

Wall, T. D., Michie, J., Patterson, M., Wood, S. J., Sheehan, M., Clegg, C. W., & West, M. (2004). On the validity of subjective measures of company performance. *Personnel psychology*, *57*(1), 95-118.

Wang, C. L. & Ahmed, P. K. (2007). Dynamic capabilities: a review and research agenda. *The International Journal of Management Reviews*, 9(1), pp. 31-51.

Wernerfelt, B. (1984). A resource_based view of the firm. *Strategic management journal*, *5*(2), 171-180.

Zhou, K.Z. & Wu, F. (2010). Technological capability, strategic flexibility, and product innovation. *Strategic Management Journal*, 31, pp. 547–561.

www.ingramcontent.com/pod-product-compliance
Lightning Source LLC
LaVergne TN
LVHW010512160826
845677LV00012B/2800

* 9 7 9 8 8 9 2 4 8 6 4 8 4 *